# The Phulasso Devotional

*Engineering the Warrior Priest for Dark Times*

## BY THURSTON D. GILL JR.

Edited by Angel R. Ackerman

**PUBLISHER'S NOTE:**

*To protect any copyright on any individual Bible translation, this devotional avoids quoting scripture. The book, chapter and verse of any verse referenced appears in the text, and in some cases, verses may be paraphrased.*

*If you do not have a Bible, verses can be found online through your favorite search engine.*

**Cover Illustration: Maryann Riker**
**Special thanks to Tiffani Velez**

If you enjoyed this book, or any book from the Parisian Phoenix roster, or any book really, consider leaving a review. Please! Reviews are an important way for small presses and independent authors to gain more traction with the all-knowing algorithms. Your review can help another reader decide to take a chance on our books! Review this book on Goodreads, Amazon and/or Google Books. Need help? Visit bit.ly/3YpKmPH or contact angel@parisianphoenix.com. To stay up-to-date with Parisian Phoenix news and to receive resources for all writers, join our Substack, *Parisian Phoenix Bookish Babble*, for our free newsletter or our subscription content.

parisian phoenix
PUBLISHING

**C O N N E C T with the publisher:**

| | |
|---|---|
| **Substack**: | parisianphoenixpublishing.substack.com |
| **Web:** | **www.ParisianPhoenix.com** |
| **Facebook** | @parisianphoenixpublishing |
| **Instagram:** | @ parisianphoenix |
| **LinkedIn** | @parisianphoenixpublishing |
| **Patreon** | @parisianphoenix |
| **TikTok** | @parisianphoenix |
| **Twitter:** | @parisbirdbooks |

# WINTER SOLSTICE

by Nancy Scott

Recycle last year's zeros
of past tense.
Write their refusal to die
in a new year's present.
Look for a poem that can bear
the survival to come.
Know that wisdom
needs practice—
the grace of loud mistakes;
the quiet courage
of knowing how to follow,
knowing how to lead,
knowing how to wait
through the long night
and the next
to learn need,
to learn want,
to learn worship.

# AUTHOR'S INTRODUCTION

This devotional collects the concepts and principles I have learned (and continue to learn) through my years of experience and observations with protecting others. These concepts and principles make up the practice of what I refer to as "Phulasso."

I hope that by sharing what's on my heart, I can fill the void regarding training in emergency preparedness mindset from a Judeo-Christian perspective.

Phulasso is an all-powers approach to personal, family, and community emergency preparedness, readiness, response, and recovery planning.

It acts as an integrated, multi-disciplinary training system to respond to multiple potential or active threats quickly, intelligently, and simultaneously with little to no support or outside resources.

All powers refers to combining our spiritual, physical, and mental powers to create a dynamic protective system to guard against potential threats to our families and communities, such as:

- Acts of Physical Violence
- Fire and Medical Emergencies
- Man-Made and Natural Disasters

Phulasso builds around protection skills that prevent, prepare for, recognize, respond to, and recover from what we refer to as critical incidents or events.

Phulasso is a Greek term borrowed from the Bible. It means to watch, to carry out the function as a military guard or sentinel (SEE ACTS 23:35, 28:16), to keep watch, to guard a person so that he might remain safe (from violence, from another person or thing, from being snatched away, from being lost).

In the New Testament, it is used as "guarding truth" (1 TIMOTHY 5:21, 6:20, 2 TIMOTHY 1:14)

In Luke 2:8, Phulasso is also a verb that describes the shepherd's "keeping watch."

Phulasso relies on a profound emphasis on the spiritual domain of operations, which means that individuals who attempt to approach this material strictly from a natural, or carnal, standpoint may be disappointed.

I aim to promote a mindset that will deepen our relationship with the resurrected Christ to enhance our understanding of the concepts and principles used to protect ourselves and others.

What I share may not contain material that some consider new and innovative. Still, many will receive a fresh revelation of spiritual truths they may not have ever realized.

Whether you are a parent, spouse, caretaker, healthcare provider, first responder, law enforcement officer, firefighter, risk manager, or security professional, or soldier, as a member of the body of Christ the magnitude of our calling requires a profoundly unique insight into the complementary capabilities that we have when ministering to others.

Our ability to protect ourselves and others is based solely on our dependence on the provisions provided by God through our Lord Jesus Christ. Without this understanding and the corresponding commitment to live it out, our protection efforts are significantly marginalized.

In other words, we're on our own!

Psalms 127:1-2 tells us that unless our faith provides the foundation for the center of our protection plans, our efforts are in vain when disaster hits.

The practice of Phulasso operates with the mind of Christ as it applies to the art and science of protecting oneself to protect others.

It is a discipline in our self-care and, as a third-party-oriented protection system, allows us to immediately intercede on behalf of others when potential threats are present or anticipated.

— Thurston D. Gill, Jr.

# DECLARATION OF PHULASSO

*As supported by Scripture*

## (THE PHULASSO MINDSET)

- "The Lord is my weapon, protection, and rescuer." (FROM 2 SAMUEL 22:3)

- He has created me to protect the weak and the poor. (PSALM 82:3-4)

- He has made me the head and not the tail. He has placed me above and not beneath. (DEUTERONOMY 28:13)

- Therefore, I can stand against all evil because the Lord is with me always. (MATTHEW 20:18-20)

# SECTION ONE:

## PREPARING YOUR MIND

# LEADERSHIP

*My competence as a leader is measured by my ability to inspire and motivate others to perform their responsibilities to standard and fulfill their purpose in this life.*

Leaders:
1. They must be held to a stricter standard than everyone else.
2. They are at greater risk of failure.
3. Have the potential to cause the most significant harm to those they represent.

Many of us in leadership struggle with expressing the courage to tell our people what we think, feel, and desire.

We are also a work in progress regarding being open to hearing and understanding their viewpoint.

Some leaders you can only half listen to, and can never follow.

Leadership is a life of service to those they are responsible for, not a life of grooming servants to take care of us.

Jesus came to serve, not to be served. (MATTHEW 20:28)

# SELF-CONTROL

## SELF CONTROL BEGINS WITH A CHRIST-RESURRECTED LIFE

The Christ-Resurrected Life refers to a life that totally lives out the power that flows from our deeply intimate relationship with the Lord Jesus. (PHILIPIANS 3:10) How do we define our powers?
- The Power of Fearlessness
- The Power of Peace
- The Power of Joy
- The Power of Confidence
- The Power of Hope
- The Power of Love
- The Power of Faith

His life becomes my nature. I no longer live but it is Christ who lives in and through me. (Galatians 2:20)

I figure if I have to work myself up to do something, that is an indication that it's not second nature and that I have not had enough practice doing it.

If we want to hone our self control and live a strongly spiritual life, it requires practice.

To gain self control within the framework of Phulasso:
- Practice living a Christ-resurrected life.
- Practice living out the knowledge that He is more significant than anything or anyone in the world.
- Practice that Christ is with us always.

## SELF-CONTROL MEANS TO WORK THE WAIT!

To me, in addition to love, there is another virtue that requires action and not mere words.

It is an elusive skill that is an offense to many of us; it is a "four letter word" that, when we are under duress and feel we need immediate relief, it's the last thing we want to hear come out of anyone's mouth.

It is the word "WAIT!"

If you are struggling with self-control, look to Lamentations 3:25-26 and pray:

>Father, please work that WAIT in me!
>Teach me not to react from my flesh but to be QUIET and respond with my WAIT!
>Please give me the mind to work my WAIT! when I care more for someone than they are willing to care for themselves.
>Teach me to perfect my WAIT! during the drama-filled epic Mondays at work.
>Teach me to perfect my WAIT! when the drama-filled epic Mondays bleed into Tuesday and Wednesday.
>Teach me to work my WAIT! when I feel powerless to come to the rescue of others.
>Please help me to work my WAIT! when I don't see immediate results after I pray for someone's healing or deliverance.
>Teach me to work my WAIT! when I have to let go of certain things because I don't have the mental, spiritual or physical energy to hold onto them.

## SELF-CONTROL MEANS ACCEPTING LACK OR LOSS

As I learn more about myself, I don't have a problem believing that God is able and willing to do whatever I can ask or even imagine.

My problem seems to be my reluctance to suffer any "lack" or "lose" until He does!

It is that "feeling" that deceptively occupies that space in time to make it seem unbearable.

The feeling of lack can transform seconds into hours and days into months in my mind!

Therefore, the issue is not precisely my lack of faith; it's my lack of patience and endurance.

*Father, please cause the precious fruit of patience and endurance to overflow in me by your grace and power.*

*It will help me to accept being without what I want when I want it calmly.*

*To be comfortable with being uncomfortable with dignity, confident that You will care for and provide for me in the name of Jesus Christ, my Lord.*

## SELF CONTROL MEANS REPROGRAMMING MY DEFAULT

By consistently practicing my spiritual disciplines, I stimulate the growth of my spiritual instincts so that I do not default to my carnal instincts.

## SELF CONTROL MEANS GETTING OUT OF MY OWN WAY

My dog Buxley's nose is usually the thing that gets him in trouble

Once he gets the scent of something, he runs headlong into The Zone of Total Impulse! He doesn't hear nor see me, no matter how much I holler and wave my hands in the air because he just doesn't care. He has temporarily forgotten that I exist.

Like Buxley, my nose can get in the way of my eyes.

My feelings get in the way of my head.

My head gets in the way of my heart.

In those moments, I have forgotten the presence of the Lord.

## SELF CONTROL MEANS MASTERING REACTIONS

My goal is to master the ability to respond to internal & external disturbances from a spiritual platform instead of with a natural, primal, base reaction. I will master my response so that I do more than react.

Follow the advice James 1:19-20: Listen carefully, speak deliberately and with reflection, monitor your own tendency toward anger, because anger will never bring us closer to our families, our fellow man, or God.

Remember Ephesians 4:26 — Acting in anger leads to trouble!

There is a difference between being angry and just plain being mean. The two need not be one. The discernment to distinguish between the two, and the discipline to avoid the latter, demonstrates my progress toward spiritual maturity.

We often profess, "I didn't mean it" when we apologize for what was said or done out of anger. This statement may or may not be the truth, but more often than not, it was definitely meant to be hurtful.

If you claim to be religious but don't control your tongue, you are fooling yourself, and your religion is worthless. (JAMES 1:26)

## SELF CONTROL MEANS FACING OUR REGRETS AND EMOTIONS

Tears do not put out the fires.

Alone, we may not be able to repair what we have broken.

We may be emotionally crushed by others correcting us.

In these moments, I tell myself, "Time to pull up my training pants, get over the regrets and trust the Lord for the power to fix it, to make it right!"

## SELF CONTROL REQUIRES EMOTIONAL ENDURANCE

I am determined never to establish anything, commit to anything, or driven to do anything that is of any lasting value based on my mood!

Disciplined to do what is right and necessary shall always be the order of the day. Because I belong to Christ, I must be resolved to endure for His sake.

These sentiments are inspired by Brother Lawrence, a Carmelite Monk in the 1600s, as recorded in The Practice of The Presence of God.

"I cannot imagine how religious persons can live satisfied without the practice of the presence of God. For my part I keep myself retired with Him in the depth of centre of my soul as much as I can; and while I am so with Him I fear nothing; but the least turning from Him is insupportable." — Brother Lawrence

How we express our emotions tells the story of how we think.

## SELF CONTROL REQUIRES MENTAL READINESS

Caring for my spiritual, emotional and physical health aligns my mind and body with my spirit to manage any situation.

## MENTAL READINESS REQUIRES SELF CONTROL OF EMOTIONS

Emotions are Holy expressions created for us by the Father. Sadly, we often weaponize them against ourselves and others. Do NOT let your emotions become the true WEAPONS OF MASS DESTRUCTION.

If I don't manage my emotions, they will manage me.
They have been known to take me to places I regret going.
They have the power to disable my logic and common sense.

## SELF CONTROL IMPROVES WITH MEDITATION/CONTEMPLATION

Once my day has begun, it takes nothing short of true grit to press the pause button for at least 15 minutes to reset, regroup and allow the Lord to refresh the screen in my head. The practice of meditation (or contemplation) transforms the WAIT! Into spiritual discipline.

## SELF CONTROL & SPIRITUAL DISCIPLINE INCLUDES CARING FOR THE BODY: NUTRITION & CONDITIONING

We all have weaknesses in self control, especially when it comes to our bodies. These five pledges apply to my relationship with my body. Make your own list, and instead of doing it for yourself or your health, dedicate your efforts to the Lord. Care for yourself so you can do His work.

1. I cannot live on physical food only. I must listen attentively to every word the Father says about my diet and His plan to keep me spiritually, mentally, and physically healthy.
2. Establish a sustainable diet that helps to control my cravings for sweets and carbs.
3. Increase intake of green leafy veggies, cauliflower, and various nuts.
4. Self-control to drink my teas without the need for sweetener.
5. Ride my bike to work daily, plus a minimum of 8,000 steps.

Now that I have more years behind me than ahead of me, I have recently become much more mindful of my nutritional and physical needs. Working my physical and nutritional disciplines requires me to work harder, not easier.

I press my way to eat nutritionally.
I force myself to maintain a strong posture.
I make the extra effort to maintain muscle tone, strength, agility, and cardiovascular endurance.

I make the effort so that I have the strength and endurance to serve others as is my duty in the eyes of the Lord.

## SELF CONTROL MEANS GROWING PAINS

Growing up requires learning to cooperate with the operation of the Holy Spirit within me, mastering the skills to manage my life's affairs without complaining or arguing my point. This is our duty as children of God. We shine only when the Father's glory works within us through the Spirit of God, and He asks that we not grumble! (PHILIPPIANS 2:13-15)

## SELF CONTROL MEANS MAINTAINING DISCIPLINED FELLOWSHIP WITH THE FATHER

Remind yourself: My motivation to persevere, to remain anchored and unshaken, becomes weak whenever my fellowship with the Father is weak. Time in His presence and the scriptures help me control my body, thoughts, and emotions.

When you are weak, return to the Father in prayer and through Scripture. Self-control means practicing discipline even when you lack motivation. This first sunk in for me in 2015. I had written the quote in my journal after reading it online: Get disciplined, not motivated. It is discipline, not motivation, that prevents giving in to temptation.

## SELF CONTROL MEANS DISCIPLINED PRAYER YIELDS EARTHLY RESULTS

Rees Howells founded the Bible College of Wales in 1924, the fledgling Christian institution surviving what is now referred to as the twentieth century's Great Depression. The success of the effort might be considered a miracle by the faithful. This man, born in 1879 in the middle of a large family (number six of eleven children), left school at age 12 to work in the coal mines and a tin mill.[1]

His life, at least according to his wife as told by Leonard Ravenhill, provides an example of self control (in the form of disciplined prayer) that yields earthly results:

"After I spoke at a session in the Bible School of Wales, Mrs. Rees Howells called me for a private talk. We stood on the veranda of her home overlooking beautiful Swansea Bay I can see her finger upheld as she said, 'Many talk of my husband's buying this place with a shilling (fourteen cents) in his pocket. What they forget is that he prayed twelve hours a day for eleven months to know the mind of God.' Brethren, that's discipline!" [2]

Ravenhill, who died in 1994, was an English, Christian evangelist and author who focused on prayer and revival. He has more than a dozen spiritual books available.

---

1 https://www.bcwales.org/legacy

2 https://www.jhopdc.com/rees-howells-part-1

## SELF CONTROL MEANS PREPARATION AND PATIENCE

We must prepare for action, gather our thoughts and our courage. As dictated in Jeremiah 1:17, do not be terrified or the Lord will terrify you.

"Get up and prepare for action. Go out and tell them everything I tell you to say. Do not be afraid of them, or I will make you look foolish in front of them."

Preparation requires self control and time. If I say I don't have time to wait, I need to examine my motivation. Is it that I don't have time, or is it really that I don't want to exercise patience?

These are two distinctly different issues.

"Patience is waiting. Not passively waiting. That is laziness. But to keep going when the going is hard and slow, that is patience. The two most powerful warriors are patience and time,"– LEO TOLSTOY.

## SELF CONTROL MEANS THE COURAGE TO WAIT

My carnal nature is the only opposition to my efforts to WAIT! on the Lord's timing. Therefore, my job is to deny my carnal nature a ballot to even to cast a vote on the matter.

Psalm 27:14 reminds us that patience in the practice of WAIT! will lead to strength rooted in the Lord.

## SELF CONTROL MEANS DEATH OF THE EGO

Dying from exposure means death resulting from lack of protection over prolonged periods to extreme temperatures, environmental conditions, or dangerous substances.
Therefore, it's good that my ego is exposed.
Lord willing, it will die of exposure.

When my defensiveness is triggered when someone holds me accountable, I allow my ego to be exposed to the light of truth so that it can die of exposure.

## SELF-CONTROL AS A TOOL AGAINST ANXIETY AND DEPRESSION

As Christians, we have extra tools when we struggle with mental health problems like anxiety and depressions. As Christians, we are never alone.

My battle with anxiety and depression has not been a once-and-done type of deliverance. They both continue to battle for space in my head and heart .

My victory over them lies in my willingness and my obedience as I work to be comfortable with being uncomfortable. My faith can work and grow only outside of my comfort zone.

What would I need with faith in Christ when I'm comfortable and safe? It's when I am not comfortable that Father can prove that He's got my back! My willingness and obedience will bring comfort if I am patient. (ISAIAH 1:19-20)

Peace will not accept my invitations to where I have already invited fear and impatience. As Jesus reminds me in John 14:27, my heart must be untroubled.

And if I turn to my spiritual roots when I feel myself worry or despair, I can weaponize music against depression and fear. (1 SAMUEL 16:14-23) In the Old Testament, God would empower musicians with the Spirit to lift the spirits of leaders facing turmoil.

Sometimes I have to ask myself, is it really a bad day, or is it that the day is not going as I planned, and I don't like it? This is the day the Lord has made. (PSALMS 118:23-24)

# STINKIN' THINKIN' ALWAYS LOOKING FOR A PLACE TO PARK.

Even as we walk with the Lord, our thoughts betray our spirituality unless we periodically clean our brains. I call this process "Mind Wash" and I use it to combat Stinkin' Thinkin'.

Pick one of these mini-meditations and contemplate it. Sit quietly with the ideas, perhaps even setting a timer for five minutes and recording your response in a journal or on a spare slip of paper to use as a bookmark in your Bible.

## MIND WASH #1
I have stopped trying to be like someone else and wanting what others have. I have no clue what others are going through or what they did to get what they got! My success will be in me doing me, because I will never be someone else. The only presence worth our emulation is that of our Creator.

## MIND WASH #2
The majority of what I used to worry about never even happened! If I find myself plagued with worry, I can turn to Proverbs 3:5-6. It reminds me that if I trust in the Lord, the path will be clear.

## MIND WASH #3
Frequent self-checks strengthen my mindfulness. If I am unsure, I can come at a situation applying the "Six Rights" (similar to the six rights of medication administration):
- Right Timing
- Right Place
- Right Solution
- Right Person (whether myself or someone else)
- Right Method
- Right Amount

## MIND WASH #4
I must (a lesson in opposites):
- Be last to be first.
- Serve to be great.
- Step blindly forward before I'm able to see.
- Decrease to increase.
- Take off to put on.
- Suffer loss in order to gain.
- Be humbled to be exalted.
- Be dumb to be wise.
- Be weak to get strong.
- Be empty to be filled.
- Give to get.

## MIND WASH #5
Commit to set aside 15-minute periods of quiet time throughout the day.

This gives me time to refresh, regroup, and revise my thoughts and plans; and to review my day.

## MIND WASH #6
I can't avoid hearing all that negativity coming at me from inside and outside of my head, but I can avoid listening to it.

MY HEAD, MY CHOICE.

## MIND WASH #7
Keep my mental diet in check. Garbage in, garbage out. Poor media programming, bad company, doom scrolling, etc.

## MIND WASH #8
I'm learning how to be a professional runner.

Quickly run from what is not good for me and run twice as hard toward what is right for me.

## MIND WASH #9
Beat up on myself less and encourage myself more!

## MIND WASH #10
My mind belongs to Christ, and I am its steward.

If I don't keep it in order, then who will?

NO EXCEPTIONS! NO EXCUSES! NO ALIBIS!

## MIND WASH #11
It's my responsibility to ensure I am using the right heart filter for hearing what people say to me.

# FAILURE TO IGNORE RELIABLE INTELLIGENCE

It is not in the DNA of our carnal nature to look at matters, especially critical issues, with our spiritual eyes, ears, and mind first and then allow our natural senses to complement them.

This requires spiritual discipline that must be practiced daily and frequently throughout the day because it is dangerous to ignore.

Our spiritual disciplines bring us to a greater degree of submission to the Spirit so that we can more fully cooperate with the will of God.

With the presence of the Holy Spirit, we possess access to "reliable intelligence" to know what is happening, what or who is behind it, and how best to deal with it.

We must always listen, and digest, because as Christians we never know when an Earthly messenger conveys the plans of our Father. (HEBREWS 12:25)

But we also must do our part to stay safe by avoiding threats and high-risk behaviors. Just because we have the Father with us does not mean we can flaunt our own safety. We must protect ourselves and act intelligently to avoid imposing this responsibility on others.

We can start by avoiding The Three Stupids, as summarized by weapons instructor and survival guru John Farnam: "Don't go to stupid places or do stupid things with stupid people.[3]" I will repeat this bit of wisdom later. It's important.

For a spiritual man/woman, operating in the spirit is tactical, and working tactically is operating in the spirit. Over time and because of use, the two become one.

---

3 https://defense-training.com/about/

# MENTAL WARFARE

In a recent article on CNN.com (October 31, 2022), I read an article that offered a quote from Jeff McCausland, an American combat veteran of the Gulf War. To me, this quote spoke to the power of infectious thought: "Fear and panic are more infectious than Covid[4]."

But the Bible gives us the tools to overcome these thoughts. There is proof that a disciplined wholesome thought process can break the yoke of addictive self-defeating feelings. It's simple really. Remember the good, the honorable, the admirable. (PHILIPPIANS 4:8)

We all have difficult thoughts from time to time but we must prevent these thoughts from becoming delusions.

Delusion: a persistent false psychotic belief regarding the self or persons or objects outside the self that is maintained despite indisputable evidence. (MERRIAM-WEBSTER COLLEGIATE DICTIONARY)[5]

We have to remind ourselves our thoughts, our delusions, are false. The Lord's grace is real.

When I recount the delusions that I have survived by the Lord's grace, it honestly concerns me that I may still be under some form of deception that keeps me blinded and in bondage to some false belief that is harmful to me and others.

Therefore, I am not only watchful, but I am careful to pray that Father helps me to identify and passionately love Truth (It fits the facts as I know it, is consistent and promotes love for Christ and others).

By loving Truth, I will be protected from the horror of maintaining any belief that would lead me to ignore it despite indisputable evidence to the contrary.

Mental clarity is important... because if you must take action, you must be certain and grounded.

## WHEN RUNNING IS NOT AN OPTION
Sometimes Father wants to give me victory but needs me to stand my ground, and after I've done everything I can to stand, STAND!

A person is only as smart (or as ignorant) as the Spirit (spirit) behind them.

---

4 https://lite.cnn.com/en/article/h_005ecd01b08ae5b6300cd9101d282ad5

5 http://merriam-webstercollegiate.com/dictionary/delusion

# PARK YOUR STINKIN' THINKIN' HERE

More of my special Mind Wash contemplations to help "put your mind right."

## STINKIN' THINKIN' #1
THOUGHT: Every time something bad happens, it's your fault.

MIND WASH: Deal with the junk in your own trunk before you step into someone else's hot mess.

## STINKIN' THINKIN' #2
THOUGHT: When the sum of your day (24 hours) has been determined by one negative encounter consisting of 30 seconds.

MIND WASH: You have successfully filtered out 23 hours, 59 minutes, and 30 seconds of blessings from your life.

## STINKIN' THINKIN' #3

**THOUGHT:** The Prophet of Doom. You exercise this gift (curse) to intuitively prophesy the worst-case scenario in EVERY situation.

**MIND WASH:** Pause. Build a gratitude list. Review your worst-case scenario and focus on what is likely, not what is possible.

## STINKIN' THINKIN' #4

**THOUGHT:** In your eyes, EVERYTHING is either chocolate or vanilla. If it ain't one of those two flavors, life is just not worth living.

**MIND WASH:** Your self-imposed blindness deprives you of the deliciousness of Tiramisu, Banana Split, Cookie Dough, Strawberry Swirl, Salted Caramel, Neopolitan, Mango...

I must challenge every thought and emotion.
 For security reasons, they are all subject to a thorough inspection.
 They will not be allowed to make me look like a fool out here in these streets!

Be like pro basketball player and humanitarian from the Democratic Republic of Congo, Dikembe Mutombo, "No, no, no." (Insert legendary finger wag here.)

# SECTION TWO:
## PREPARING FOR A FIGHT

# PRINCIPLES OF PERSONAL PROTECTION

Now that we have explored the internal, emotional challenge of setting our mind right in the eyes of the Lord, we can move into Principles of Personal Protection as possible through the practice of Phulasso.

Our strategy is to achieve rapid & total tactical superiority in all spiritual, mental, and physical domains against all threats.

## PHULASSO OPERATIONAL MODEL

When the Lord wants to get something done, His model is often, "Less is more."
   When faced with a superior enemy force, one might prefer the sense of security they may get with a bunch of guns and gun buddies that are trained to handle them or the best rescue equipment along with the best-trained rescuers.

   But under the circumstances like these, more often than not, the Lord says to His children, that His grace is sufficient; take what is in hand right now, and fewer men than those that are with you right now, and you will advance, because you have the Lord with you! If the Lord can feed a crowd with two fish, he will surely provide for you. There are many occasions in the Bible where a Believer defeats his oppressor. (2 CORINTHIANS 12:9, JOHN 6:9, JUDGES 7:7, DEUTERONOMY 1:8, KINGS 6:16-18)

## HARD-WIRING A NEW DEFAULT

I am strict about spiritual disciplines because it helps to develop my instincts, so I do not default to my old carnal instincts. Similar to developing our mental and emotional framework, we need to rewire our brains against previous detrimental thinking habits.

## IN ANY CONFLICT, END IT QUICKLY

A prolonged fight is generally a lost fight. When you go into battle you want to put your enemies down as fast as possible. We should never allow any enemies—the World, Flesh, or the Devil—to drag out the battle, because you will eventually wear down and lose the fight.

Once it is triggered, I am driven to end the conflict quickly. Time does NOT work in my favor for several reasons; therefore, I MUST control the tempo and finish it soon as possible.

For further reading, see *Mighty Men: Lessons for the Christian Soldier; A Biblical look at David's Mightiest Men* by Stephen C. Roberts.

## USE THE RIGHT WEAPON, SWIFTLY!

Consider the words of Bruce Lee, world-renowned martial arts legend: "There's only one basic principle of self-defense—you must apply the most effective weapon, as soon as possible, to the most vulnerable target."

At first blush, this made total sense to me. But after more time to consider the statement more deeply, it seems to me that this is only accurate if all the boxes in the "6 Rights"(remember them from our last section) are checked:

- Right Solution
- Right Time
- Right Place
- Right Person
- Right Way
- Right Amount

## MAKE 'EM WORK FOR IT!

If it's Father's will that I die protecting myself or others, so be it! What authority do I have to oppose His will in this matter?

I will submit myself to our Lord and resist all other opposing forces, spiritual or natural.

## I AM DETERMINED TO MAKE MYSELF AND THOSE AROUND ME TO BE EXTREMELY DIFFICULT TO HURT OR KILL!

## EMPLOY ADAPTIVE DEFENSE

My definition of adaptive defense: The full use of the environmental conditions, my motivation under the current circumstances, and the enemy's weaknesses to launch a counter-ambush response to render myself and others safe.

## BE AWARE OF THE NEW & DIFFERENT

Threats are subject to change. Often, the threat adjusts in response to new or different security measures. I must always be receptive to additional or new information, then act accordingly.

## ADAPT TO THE FLOW OF AGGRESSION

Prussian military commander Helmuth von Moltke the elder, one of the influential figures in designing modern warfare, said that "no plan survives the first contact with the enemy." But strategies do.

I can't anticipate every possibility in a violent or non-violent encounter, so it is not wise to put my total confidence in one canned response.

I must be ready to Adapt as the Spirit leads me.

## TACTICAL OPTIONS VS. LEGAL STRATEGIES

CCTV cameras can be valuable tools to assist in an attacker's capture and (possible) conviction. CCTV cameras exemplify a viable strategic tool in the judicial and law enforcement process to execute justice.

But unless those cameras are operated and monitored in such a way as to detect, deter, or activate an immediate response to an attack, it could never be considered a tactical option.

## REVELATION & RECOGNITION

A revelation of what is happening in a situation does not automatically trigger recognition of what's going on. Sometimes, we can be in denial.

For whatever reason, the situation may not be real to me. I may be in denial, or I may rebel against the truth.

## CONTEXT DICTATES RESPONSE

I must always consider the entirety of what's going on before committing to an action. One particular response won't fit every situation. Consequently, my response doesn't need to change just because the situation changes.

## SELF CONTROL AS PROTECTION

Self control protects me from unnecessary exposure to harm.

By denying myself the opportunity to engage in at-risk behaviors, I minimize the threat of getting my clock cleaned physically and spiritually. Proverbs 25:28 compares a man without self control to a house left wide open. Self control allows you to lock the door and close the windows.

In other words, in the words of weapons instructor and survival guru John Farnham, "Avoid the Three Stupids. Don't go to stupid places or do stupid things with stupid people."[5]

---

5 https://defense-training.com/about/

## MY FIGHTS ARE FIXED– IN MY FAVOR
The awareness of Father's presence builds my strength and my courage. I am not dependent on hype that comes from bravado or propaganda. The Lord will not fail me. Nothing separates me from the Lord, nothing in all of God's creation. (DEUTERONOMY 31:6, ROMANS 8:38-39)

The Lord says that when I am under attack, He is my:
1. Platform (on which I fight from)
2. Fortress of Protection
3. Rescuer
4. Strength
5. Safe Haven
6. Salvation
7. Protection against the Ruthless

And if that's not enough, He told me that every fight is fixed in my favor! (2 SAMUEL 22:2-4)

## THE IMPORTANCE OF BEING SENSITIVE TO THE SPIRIT
Just because I naturally react to threats in a certain way does not mean it is the right thing to do at a given time.

I must listen and respond to the Spirit's promptings. He knows what I need to do at any given time, especially during a critically emergent event.

## CAPABILITIES OVER KNOWLEDGE
A person whose only strength is their knowledge of the rule of law is of little value to me when I am fighting for my life or the life of another.

A person who can quickly recognize when the rules change and have the capability and the will to govern themselves accordingly is of infinitely more value to me.

## COUNTER-AMBUSH
When the attacker has the upper hand, I master the art of reshuffling the deck. I must not allow him to control the deck.

I strive to master the ability to do the unexpected; this enables me to control the conflict better.

## THE CONSEQUENCES OF POOR JUDGMENT
When predators decide to strike, they expect the behavior of prey. Whether me or mine is targeted, I make it clear that they are sadly mistaken.

## DON'T FIGHT THEIR FIGHT; FIGHT MINE!

I try not to fight anyone else's style of combat. Father has taught my hands how to war, and my fingers how to fight according to the fight He has selected for me to win. I will follow in the steps of David. (PSALM 144)

## THE OUT-MANEUVER

The winner of a violent encounter will be whoever has the most foresight and intuition to out-counter the other. The Holy Spirit is my advisor in these matters. I must trust the Spirit.

## PASS OR FAIL

There is no grading system in combat. So I either pass or fail.

**I SURVIVE TODAY TO FIGHT AGAIN FOR SOULS TOMORROW.**

**TRAIN TO BE HARD: HARD TO STOP, HARD TO KILL**

## THE PROPER ORDER

Spiritual and Technical Intelligence comes before physical ability. Physical ability can NEVER compensate for the absence of the other two.

## THE TRIPLE THREAT

**SKILLS**

If I have excellent skills but fall short of awareness or resolve, I lose!

**AWARENESS**

If I don't see the attack coming to avoid it or see it is time to counter, I lose!

My resolve doesn't matter; my skills don't matter! AWARENESS BEATS SKILLS AND RESOLVE.

Even though I see it coming and can put some hurt to him with my skills, if the attacker is more determined to kill me than I am committed to living, I lose! RESOLVE CAN BEAT AWARENESS AND SKILLS.

## THE BAD GUY GETS TO VOTE, TOO!

No matter my plans concerning defending others or myself from an attack, I must remember that the bad guy gets a vote.

My job is to make sure that their vote doesn't count.

## OVER-ESTIMATE THE BAD GUY
I prefer being surprised at how weak and inexperienced my attacker is rather than waking up in a hospital bed, wondering what happened.

## FAITH, CONFIDENCE, AND TRUST
Confidence in my training comes from practice, and trust in my equipment comes from testing. A battle won easily is a confidence builder, but faith is only developed when we engage in battles that are high risk, hard fought and costly. Confidence fuels my skills and attitude about climbing up the mountain, while faith enables me to move the mountain altogether.

## OFF THE RADAR
The most challenging target to attack is the target that is undetectable.

## SOMETHING IS BETTER THAN NOTHING
If I gotta hit someone, It's better to do it with something— preferably something hard & heavy— than with nothing at all.

## SMOOTH IS FAST, AND FAST IS SMOOTH!
*Festina Lente*, the classical adage in Italian, means literally "make haste slowly."

## CONTROL MY BATTLESPACE!
STAY CLOSE, AND STRIKE OFTEN until the attacker has no more fight in him.

## DEFENSIVE TARGETING STRATEGY
**Target:** Respirations, Vision, Mobility, Structure, and Consciousness
If we make it so that the attacker is:
- Unable to BREATHE normally
- Unable to SEE
- Unable to maintain CONSCIOUSNESS
- Unable to STAND
- Unable to maintain MOBILITY of their limbs

**WE HAVE EFFECTIVELY REMOVED THE FIGHT FROM THEM!**

## WHEN TO STOP FIGHTING

When I am fighting for my life or the lives of others, as a "PHYLAKAS" (or guardian), It is important for me to understand that after a battle begins when I am PERMITTED to stop fighting. It's not:

- When I am injured. Jeremiah 17:14 reminds us that the Lord heals and saves. I praise the Lord and rely on him.

- When I am exhausted. Isaiah 40:31 reminds us that the Lord will give us strength and energy.

- When I am hungry or thirsty. Deuteronomy 8:3 tells us that the Lord will feed us, via our bellies and our souls. We live through the Lord.

- When I am afraid or outnumbered. Deuteronomy 20:1 reminds us that the Lord is always with us and that his power is always greater than that of our enemies. He will deliver us.

- When I am fighting alone. Joshua 1:9 tells is not to fear or get discouraged for when I value my relationship with the Lord, he will always be by my side.

- When I am sad or grieving. Psalm 34:18 reminds us that the Lord will always comfort those who are broken—in heart or in spirit.

- When an ally betrays me. Psalm 55 reminds us that when we follow the Lord, even when friends stab us in the back, the Lord will not let us fall.

In other words, if I have faith in the Lord, I HAVE ALREADY WON THE BATTLE. That is not the issue!

All I have to do is "NOT QUIT" until this fact is communicated to my enemy in a way they understand.

# SITUATIONAL AWARENESS

## AWARENESS ALLOWS ME TIME.

## TIME ALLOWS ME OPTIONS

The skills that integrate the mastery of Timing, Distance, Balance and Speed are wasted without Situational Awareness. Situational Awareness provides the options to use these skills.

I cannot ignore the danger, or evil, around me. I must prepare myself. Those who ignore what is happening around them will pay the price. (PROVERBS 27:12)

The ability to perceive threats far off and close up is essential.

I am not supposed to be able to discern everything that happens around me. I am expected to trust Father to discern what is important for me to see and know. (2 CORINTHIANS 5:7)

To better understand how people think, I focus an unbiased eye on their actions rather than my ears to their words.

Naturally, the leopard's eye is on the goat, and the eye of the goat is naturally on the leaf. Still, suppose that goat continues to only focus its eye on what it naturally tends to do at the expense of what is tactically practical given the current circumstances. In that case, it will not go well for him.

My level of vulnerability is closely related to my level of awareness.

If I don't see the attack coming to avoid it or see it is time to counter, I lose! My resolve doesn't matter, and my skills don't matter!

Awareness can help me avoid danger, so I don't have to use skills and resolve. (PROVERBS 27:12)

More often than not, a person who knows how to use the element of surprise and has the resolve to survive has the potential to overcome an opposing force with superior skills.

The winner of a violent encounter is usually the one with the most foresight and/or intuition to out-counter the other.

# SECURITY

## QUALITY SECURITY IS INCONVENIENT.
If our security measures are designed to be convenient for us, then we have most likely made it even more convenient for those that mean us harm.

## THINK AND LIVE TACTICALLY
Life and living are full of opposing forces.

It requires that I acquire and maintain a tactical position quickly and consistently. As Christians, we wrestle with a variety of Earthly and Spiritual powers, but we wear the armor of God. (EPHESIANS 6:11-12)

## FLEXIBILITY IS NOT OPTIONAL
Security operations must be form-fitting to the needs of those who require protection. Operations must flex, expand, and contract according to the nature of the potential threats.

## THE HUMAN ENEMY
The greatest threat to any group's security has always been people. Whether the threats are physical or spiritual, as a result of unintentional human frailty or malicious intent, theft, death, and destruction have been allowed access to victims through a person.

## HOLDING MY GROUND
Man's might and power will always be limited. The omnipotence of God, on the other hand, backs the person who holds their ground with moral integrity. That person has access to whatever muscle from Heaven is needed to get the win!

## FATHER HAS AN ENTIRELY DIFFERENT PERSPECTIVE
When faced with a superior enemy force, we become desperate for some sense of security.

But under the circumstances like these, more often than not, the Lord says to His children, "my grace is sufficient, take what you have in hand right now, and fewer than those that are with you now and don't just hold your ground, I command you to advance, because more are with you than those that are with them!" This is a common theme in Biblical stories.

## AND REMEMBER...THE FIGHT IS ALWAYS FIXED IN MY FAVOR
The Lord reminds me that there will always be a fight and that He will be with me ALWAYS!

## SAFETY & SECURITY SKILLS

**WISDOM (Combative Skills)**—Allows the domain of my inner man to be engaged in both kinetic & non-kinetic combative scenarios.

**KNOWLEDGE (Cunning Awareness)**—Gives me mental stability and peace of mind. A faithful companion that will scout out ahead of me.

**DISCRETION & UNDERSTANDING (Tactical Decision-Making)**— They work together to watch over and protect me. (PROVERBS 2:10-15)

If our security measures aren't prevention & deterrent driven initiatives, then it is not security.

# IN SUMMARY... IF FACED WITH
# A PHYSICAL THREAT

### KEEP IT MOVIN'
When chaos is having way too much fun, I have to move it along in the name of Jesus!

### END THE FIGHT QUICKLY!
A prolonged fight is generally a lost fight. When you go into battle you want to put your enemies down as fast as possible. We should never allow any enemies—the World, Flesh, or the Devil—to drag out the battle because you will eventually wear down and lose the fight. (EPHESIANS 6:10-12)

For further reading, see *Mighty Men: Lessons for the Christian Soldier; A Biblical Look at David's Mightiest Men* by Stephen C. Roberts

### REALITY CHECK
I must remain connected with the reality that there are three realms in which I must be operational:

**NATURAL:** Here on Earth.

**SPIRITUAL:** Here in Earth's atmosphere where angelic and demonic beings operate. This is where I am to conduct warfare in the spirit.

**HEAVEN:** The Throne of the Father resides here, and the Lord Jesus rules. Heaven is the seat of my power, where I obtain the authority and the ability to operate in the other two realms.

### WORKING THE PUNK OUT OF ME
This is how the Lord works that punk out of me! As I face and not back down from trials and my enemies, he makes me (and my Faith) stronger! (JAMES 1:2-4)

### KNOWING HOW TO CHOSE MY BATTLES
I discovered that learning to choose my battles wisely is an essential life skill that can save your life on the streets and help preserve your sanity at home, work, and school.

### ANGRY VS. MEAN
I said it earlier and I'll repeat it here. There is a difference between being angry and just plain being mean. The two need not be one. The discernment to distinguish between the two, and the discipline to avoid the latter, demonstrates my progress toward spiritual maturity. Act only when you are calm and rational. (EPHESIANS 4:26)

## STRENGTHS & WEAKNESSES
My strength is in my weakness; my weakness is reliance on my power instead of Father's provision. With my total surrender and submission to Father's will, I forfeit my will and power to the His.

## BRIEF MOMENTS
Brief moments of despair can't be allowed to dictate the overall quality of my life.

## CONQUER THE BEAST
I conquer this beast; all other beasts will fall before me! But we must remember, we are more than merely conquerers. (ROMANS 8:37)

## MISSED OPPORTUNITIES
Before I start grieving over missed opportunities that I blame others for, I take a peek in my rear view mirror and remember the opportunities I single-handedly messed up on my own. (You might want to read that one again.)

# SECTION THREE:

## PREPARING FOR EMERGENCIES

# EMERGENCY PREPAREDNESS

## PHULASSO OPERATIONAL MODEL

When the Lord wants to get something done, His model is often, "Less is more."

When faced with a superior enemy force, one might prefer the sense of security one may have with a bunch of guns and gun buddies that are trained to handle them; or more rescue equipment and more trained rescuers.

In each section of this book, the same concept reappears.

It's the same under the circumstances like these, more often than not, the Lord says to His children, "my grace is sufficient; take what you have in hand right now, and fewer than those that are with you right now, and don't just hold your ground, on the contrary, I command you to advance, because more are with you than those that are with them!" (2 CORINTHIANS 12:9, JOHN 6:9, JUDGES 7:7, DEUTERONOMY 1:8, KINGS 6:16-18)

I try to remember that whenever I find myself involved in a critical event that is a threat to my safety and the safety of others that I am meant to be there! I am in harm's way for a purpose: to intercede on behalf of those involved.

For both villains & victims.

So I must:

ALWAYS BE READY, MANNED-UP AND DETERMINED TO DO MY JOB!

All things work together to fulfill the will of God. (ROMANS 8:27-28)

Father gives me insight and understanding and enhances my capabilities through my spiritual disciplines. But it is through the hardships and trauma that He has tempered my preparedness into readiness to care for others in emergencies and other critical events.

When I respond to safety or security emergencies, I do my part to prepare for service. Still, it is Father's grace that compensates for what I don't have or don't know. That is Amazing Grace.

## ALL POWERS: TOTALLY ALIGNED

Utilizing all of my powers to protect others requires a total alignment of my mind and body with my spirit to manage any situation. The absence of either renders me ineffective in that particular domain.

## RELATIONAL POWER AND AUTHORITY

The height, width, and depth of my relationship with the Lord Jesus determine my operational effectiveness in the field. The Lord gives me the authority to defeat my enemy, or trample the scorpions. And that authority also means I shall bring others to strengthen their relationship to the Lord. (LUKE 10:19, MATTHEW 28:18-20)

## MUCH MORE THAN MY GEAR

I pray that none of us are seduced into thinking that our survival gear is the answer to our survival problems. If we do, it is clear we need to understand the basic principles of survival and how to use our gear so that we don't place ourselves and those we hope to protect in danger.

## DEVELOPING MY SPIRITUAL INSTINCTS

Spiritual Disciplines promote the growth of my spiritual instincts, so I do not default to my carnal instincts.

## FALSE IMPRESSIONS

Many people, whether they know it or not, have the skills to survive a violent encounter, but far too many don't have the skills to win one. The sad truth is that they are convinced that they do. The fewer skills you have, the more problems you can expect to have.

## MY HERITAGE

As children of God, we operate under the powers of our heritage. These powers are:

- Love
- Peace
- Righteousness
- Security

And we will have victory over any opposition that threatens any of the above. (ISAIAH 54:14-17)

## TOP PRIORITY

In terms of survivability, Safety & Security supersedes all earthly needs.

## MY LEVEL OF ENGAGEMENT
Spirit-led discretion always determines the level of my engagement with threats.

## KNOWING MY OPTIONS
Total Awareness is necessary to identify or create various options to survive any crisis event. It helps me orient to what, when, where, who and why.

## EXPECT THE UNEXPECTED AND ADAPT QUICKLY.

## THE LAW OF REDUNDANCY
When emergency prepping food, supplies, and equipment, always have more than enough so that Murphy's Law doesn't leave you holding air:

Three is two, two is one, and one is none.

That is, if you start with three and lose one, you still have two, one for you and one to share.

But if you start with two and lose one, you also have one to share.

If you start with just one and lose it, you have none left, none for you nor any for anyone else.

## THE ABSENCE OF PROPER PLANNING
A panicked and confused reaction to an emergency is evidence that proper planning is absent. When God is present, peace follows. If you do not keep God at the center, confusion results. (1 CORINTHIANS 14:33)

## NO QUICK FIX
Surviving and winning in a survival scenario requires long, ongoing, and persistent preparation.

## I AM THE TOOL OF SERVICE
I am not the Carpenter. I may be the hammer, sometimes the nail, but never the craftsman.

I don't have the power within to fix anything, nor the ability to create, but the Carpenter (THE LORD JESUS) does.

I am happy to serve as a tool of the Lord.

## BE AT PEACE WITH MY PART

The wrong and the level of evil inflicted on people in this world often overwhelms me.

I often feel powerless against the magnitude of what I can do to help correct some of the consequences of The Fall.

We need to counterbalance our feelings of despair:
- What's the use?
- Nothing I can do.
- I give up!
- It's just too big or too far or for too long unchecked.

It bothers me because I do care!

**I MUST FIND THE PEACE IN DOING MY PART!**
**IF THERE IS PEACE; I HAVE TO ACCEPT IT!**

We all have a duty to do our best to prepare for our battles, but we all must rely on the Lord.

In a catastrophic incident, many people are convinced that they would fare better in the wilderness than in an urban or suburban environment because of the threat of large amounts of people.

The reality is that in the woods, the danger of other people still does exist, but not in the same amount as in more populated areas.

It's just that the entirety of creation is determined to hurt and kill us in the wilderness, and we'd better have the required skills to manage it.

The more time I spend in the wilderness, the more skills, experience, and sound judgment are required to remain safe.

Be prepared for the unexpected!
It was always the ones we didn't see coming that got us.

Preparation/Readiness is our deductible for the insurance of the Lord's protection during a crisis. (PROVERBS 21:31)

## TACTICAL COMMUNICATION

Tactical Communication: Verbal and non-verbal skill sets that are used to interact with people who are in various stages of aggressive behaviors.

# INFLUENCES: FACTS & FEELINGS

One is influenced more by what makes sense and another by what they feel. Neither is right nor wrong.

The logic that disregards emotions has the potential to be harmful; emotions without reason have the potential to be toxic as well.

Wisdom says it is often senseless to debate with the Irrational, Unreasonable, and Impossible.

When someone fails to control their crazy, it should only expose my ability to control mine. This keeps me and mine safe.

## OWNERSHIP IN BEING MISUNDERSTOOD
I am learning to take more responsibility for being understood by others.

## I STILL WIN
During a crisis, spiritual wellness makes all the difference in my outcome. Whether I physically don't perform well during a crisis doesn't matter as long as I prioritize that which is eternal over the temporal, that which is spiritual over the worldly or fleshly. As long as my spiritual wellness remains intact, I will always be more than a conqueror in Christ.

## THE GIFT OF TALK
"If you can't protect yourself with talk, you won't be alive to protect yourself with guns."– AUSTRALIAN ARTIST ARTHUR BOYD

## RATIONAL COMMUNICATION
It makes more sense to me to take criticism and other negative behaviors from others to the head, not to the heart. The heart is way too sensitive to evil, ignorance & stupidity.

When given the opportunity, the head can handle it. It challenges the illogical with logic and nonsense with sensibility.

On the other hand, emotions can escalate the matter and delay a resolution.

The heart can trigger an emotional reaction.

The head can trigger a reasonable response

## DIFFUSING CRAZY
Wisdom teaches that a peace offering given quietly can often defuse crazy. And that gifts work better than bribes. (PROVERBS 21:14)

## ON LISTENING
When I listen to others in conversation, it helps me to clarify and to express my thoughts. Sometimes, I must initiate or feed the conversation, but my objective is to LISTEN! I will only know what to say if I am listening to what is being said.

## SKILLED IN UNDERSTANDING
The Holy Spirit helps me to practice advanced communication skills. These skills enable me to interpret what a person means (no matter what they are verbally saying). It also helps them because they may need help understanding what they mean, too.

## DEDICATION OF PRESENCE
A time dedicated to total engagement, no distractions, and no wondering of thought, can prevent or defuse many conflicts.

## BULLYING BEHAVIOR
From my personal experience, managing conflicts by aggressively intimidating others into compliance instead of trying to find out how I can contribute to the peace usually results in viewing others as incompetents who need to be saved from themselves.

Intimidation is not a tactical communication skill. This is referred to as bullying.

## PROJECTED PEACE
I will only know that I have peace if there is a disturbance to challenge it; I will only know if I can project it if there is conflict.

The peace that flows from my relationship with Jesus Christ promotes security, safety, and prosperity.

In Chaos, MY SPACE IS ORDER
In Crisis, MY SPACE IS PEACE

In times of chaos I pray: *Father, please help me to perfect the art of being brief and precise.*

## AVOIDING TRIGGERS
During a disagreement, asking honest questions in the right way can often encourage the other person and me to think about our points or decisions without triggering our defensiveness.

Whenever our defensive triggers are activated, we are not in a good place to listen to each other.

## CHOOSING MY BATTLES

I discovered that choosing battles worth fighting is an essential life skill that can save my life on the streets and help preserve my sanity at home, work, and school.

## 5 REASONS TO DEVELOP MY DE-ESCALATION SKILLS

1. They reduce the risk of death or injury to myself and others.
2. Mitigate Legal Liability. The government and a jury may not perceive the aggressor as a legitimate threat as I do.
3. Physical or mental limitations. Environmental conditions, my mental/physical condition, or poor visibility may give an aggressor more of an advantage than I care to provide for them.
4. Outnumbered and outgunned. Wisdom may dictate that I fight another day, another way.
5. I honestly don't get any pleasure in hurting others. Every time I have to do it, it takes something from me that I can't quite explain.

## THE TRUTH IS STRONG ENOUGH TO SUPPORT ITSELF

The Lord showed me that I need to let the truth stand on its own.

Anything I do to alter it to fit what I want, I am in error, regardless of the sincerity of my motives. Any changes I make to it causes it to cease to be the truth.

## KNOWLEDGE MANAGEMENT

I am not responsible for sharing what the Lord doesn't show me, only for what He does.

I am responsible for sharing only what He tells me and only when He allows me to share it.

I am not held responsible for sharing what He says with everyone, but I am expected to share with those who are meant to hear.

## I CAN'T SEE ALL OF ME

My perspective of myself is limited.

As I relate to others, I must be mindful that there are 360 degrees of perspective about me.

There are sides and angles of my being that I am not mindful of on my own.

I must consider the input of others about what they observe.

## TAKING OWNERSHIP OF LISTENING

It's my responsibility to ensure I am using the right heart filter to listen to what people say or do not say during a conflict.

## STAY IN MY LANE
Wisdom teaches me that when I am limited in understanding, it may not be the time to offer my opinion. Fools delight in their own opinions. (PROVERBS 18:2)

## THE FAVOR OF GOD, THE RESPECT OF OTHERS
Growing up is operating under the Holy Spirit's influence to manage my life's affairs without complaining and the impulse to argue my point. Through my relationship with Christ, I will shine regardless of the nature of the people around me. (PHILIPPIANS 2:13-15)

## LESS OF ME MEANS MORE OF CHRIST
I am working on perfecting the art of saying less, not saying more. I realize that the fewer but more impactful words that come out of my mouth, the more people hear the heart of Christ.

## GIVING AWAY MY OATS
In all of my interactions with others, I must CONVEY that I am:
Open
Attentive
Tolerant
Safe

## THE RIGHT QUESTIONS
Asking the right question is often the key to many solutions. When I ask the "right" questions, I encourage people to think about their point or decision instead of triggering a defense.

## MY RIGHTS AND THE CONSIDERATION OF OTHERS
I have learned that just because a person respects my right to have an opinion doesn't mean that they appreciate hearing it.

## CONFLICTS ARE UNCOMFORTABLE BUT HELPFUL
My understanding is that the reason why I find myself involved in conflicts is that the Lord wants to change ME and EVERYONE involved!

## TACTICAL PLANNING & DECISION-MAKING

If the sum of my decisions tends to be only for my benefit, then self-centeredness is my focus.

If the sum of my decision tends to be entirely on the needs of others at the expense of my self-care, self-centeredness is still my focus.

Using the needs of others to satisfy my need to be needed is called ministering to get my needs met.

The Holy Spirit helps me to prioritize the needs I should be concerned about because He is my service manager.

The Spirit has access to know everything He needs to determine what needs to be done. (1 CORINTHIANS 2:10-11)

## VALUE OF LIFE EXPERIENCE

The Father's hidden concepts and principles are embedded in all my life experiences.

Whether these experiences are good, bad, principal, or minor, the Holy Spirit enables me to develop them into practical tools that I use intuitively to deal with various situations.

## ONE TRUE VOICE

I don't need to listen to every voice to determine which one is true.

I only have to submit myself to be conditioned to recognize the One Voice I need to listen to.

When warnings come, I must heed them. (HEBREWS 12:25)

## WHEN I MAKE DECISIONS...

....I will operate in what I know while trusting the Lord to make up the difference in what I lack in everything else.

...to protect myself and others, I must quickly know what rules apply to specific situations and recognize when no rules apply at all.

...responding to high-risk situations, CONTEXT ALWAYS MATTERS! I must always consider and understand what's going on before committing to any action (verbal or physical).

## SHARE THE WEIGHT

We as humans and the situations we find ourselves in are waaaaay too complicated to think that any one specific response will work for every situation. Therefore, it is quite a challenge for me to roll the weight of the responsibility of how to respond on the Father's shoulders, but learn I must.

## HUMAN LIMITS

My limited human thinking leaves far too much room for error, and I have far too many years behind me than ahead of me to screw up what time I have left.

I need my remaining years to be results-oriented.

With the Lord as my focus, I will find success. God's plans succeed.

(PROVERBS 16:3, 19:21)


For help discerning the Lord's plans, I pray:

> *Holy Spirit, please direct us so that we see things in the "Right*
> *Context" and protect us from ourselves and from others who*
> *mean us harm by helping us to do the*
> *"Right" things to the Right people,*
> *at the Right time,*
> *in the Right place,*
> *with the Right solution, delivered in the Right way,*
> *in the Right amount,*
> *with the Right motives.*
> *In Jesus's name.*
> *Thank you, Father.*


When I don't know what to do next, I master what I am already doing until the Lord opens up the next window of opportunity for another.

Our mastery of the one often prepares us for the opening of the next.

## FATHER GOD'S JOB

To give me:
1. Discernment
2. Knowledge
3. Understanding

MY JOB
1. To make the Decision
2. To execute Action

If my plan didn't work, that's awesome!!!
That means there is an opportunity for the Lord's plan to work!

I get it! Some things are not clearly black and white, but I am not blind
to the fact that what God has painted black and white can't be colored
any other way.

> "If you keep souls as your number one priority, you will never
> be out of the will of God." –LESTER SUMRALL,
> AMERICAN PENTECOSTAL PASTOR AND EVANGELIST

I believe the Word of the Lord when He says that no matter what happens,
He can make it work to benefit those who love him because they have a purpose, and he has a plan. (ROMAN 8:28) Nonetheless, I am just as convinced that
whatever starts wrong, without His grace, usually ends wrong!

The Lord wraps my personality around His ideas. The wrapping is of little
value compared to the content inside. I must be careful not to regard the
wrapping at the expense of the contents.

I also learned that there will be times when I just have to, in the words of
Michael Stephen Fuchs the author of the Arisen series, military special operations novels,"take that flashlight off my pocket knife," trust God, "and take a
stab in the dark."

The right question is often the key to many solutions.

When I am too busy in my daily misdirected activities, I can't detect the
gentle current of the Holy Spirit.

Common sense is only common to those who share the same reference point.

I am determined never to establish anything, commit to anything, or be coerced to do anything that is of any lasting value based on my mood!

My motivation to do what is right and necessary shall always be the order of the day.

One aspect of living a Spirit-filled life is learning not to rely entirely on my senses!

I am in lifelong training not to assume anything that the Holy Spirit has not revealed.

It's safer that way.

Some of my past experiences may no longer be valuable tools for the present situation.

Like manna, the usefulness of what happened yesterday has a short shelf-life.

I need today's revelation, today's anointing, today's portion of grace, today's teaching, today's mercy, today's…

It's too easy to judge people and situations by our senses (which, by the way, are easily deceived).
But then again, when people show us who they are, we still don't believe it!

It's easier to be led by the flesh than to learn to submit to the leading of the Holy Spirit to get to the root of a matter.

# TYPES OF TOXIC LOGIC

The Holy Spirit allows me to be aware of the following supposed forms of logic:

## SHALLOW LOGIC
Thinking that does not take into consideration the totality of the circumstance.

## DISTORTED LOGIC
An inappropriate or unreasonable way of thinking about something that has been intentionally altered for the purpose of convincing others that it is reasonable and appropriate.

## DYSFUNCTIONAL LOGIC
The ability to think reasonably and appropriately is impaired or functions abnormally.

## BROOM LOGIC
Reasoning that makes quick, sweeping generalizations without any factual support.

## HOLY SPIRIT LOGIC
During my initial engagement in any crisis, I can never assume more than I do. The situation is still too fresh and too new for me to do that.

Many decisions must be made without having the luxury of waiting to get a clear understanding of what's going on. In those moments, I rely upon the Holy Spirit's direction to pilot the way.

Nevertheless, I consciously try to understand what's going on, way before coming to any conclusion or prescribing a resolution to the matter.

Understanding can often cast more light on an otherwise shaded situation.
(PROVERBS 4:7)

Emmanuel (God with Me)
>*Where I go, Christ goes.*
>*When I speak, He hears.*
>*When I think, He sees.*
>*When I feel, He knows.*

## GODLY RESULTS REQUIRES GODLY THINKING

My tactical planning and decision-making only work when I invest the time to think with Father and execute action with the mind of Christ.

When I spend time with Him, I understand His plans and how He works.

I will instantaneously know what to do before, during, and after a critical event because I am attuned to Father's will and planning. (COLOSSIANS 1:19, 2 CORINTHIANS 2:15-16)

The ability to make good decisions comes from experience and experience from making many bad and sound decisions.

With enough experience making good and bad decisions in a given area, I have become much better at making intuitive decisions.

# UPGRADE THE TOOLS IN MY TOOLBOX AND THE SKILLS TO USE THEM

When my only tools are a screwdriver and a hammer, there will always be a tendency to look at every problem as a screw or a nail.

Tactical Decision-Making is simply making tough decisions, with minimal information, in fractions of seconds, sometimes with lives hanging in the balance. Then LIVING WITH IT.

## IS GOOD DECISION-MAKING ONLY OUTCOME BASED?
I can't always judge how good a decision is based on only the outcome –
I believe the value of a decision should be based on what we know at the time.

If we knew in advance how the situation would work out, all our decisions would be perfect.


## LISTENING FOR DIRECTION
No matter how much I see or have been told of a situation, I will always have a deficit of complete knowledge of what is happening.

I must trust the Lord. He sees and knows the entire area of operation and everyone and everything in it.

Therefore, I must never compromise doing what is right; stick to righteousness, integrity, and honor, and I will be okay.

That's where Father will meet me. (PROVERBS 3:5-7)

# CRISIS MANAGEMENT & RECOVERY

Crisis reveals the hidden HEROES!

A person's spiritual and mental orientation often determines their capability to recover from a crisis.

The course of my life consists of the following:
• The Unexpected
• The Unexplainable
• The Unthinkable
• The Uncontrollable
I NEED ALL OF JESUS!!

## THE SOVEREIGNTY OF TRUTH
It is the truth that I must allow to govern my thoughts and actions.
By understanding and applying truth to what is currently happening in my life will keep me safe. The truth sets us free. (JOHN 8:31-32)

Father has given me the grace to think tactically and the ability to maneuver my way through any situation with confidence and skill, efficiency, and effectiveness...

• NO MATTER HOW LONELY
• NO MATTER HOW UNCOMFORTABLE
• NO MATTER HOW MUCH IT HURTS
• NO MATTER HOW SCARY
• NO MATTER HOW OVERWHELMING
   ... the crisis may be.

## CRISIS RESPONSE HANDBOOK
If we need a "Crisis Response Handbook," we should turn to the Bible.

For example, Paul and Silas were unjustly imprisoned because God used them to deliver a slave girl who her masters and a demonic spirit were exploiting.

Obeying God resulted in cruel and painful flogging and imprisonment in the worst section of the jail.

Both men had a strong legal and moral claim to protest and lodged a wrongful arrest and corporal punishment complaint. Instead, they chose to trust the Lord in their circumstances, evidenced by their praise.

As a result of their **faith** and **praise** to the Lord, the **power** of God showed up to physically release them from prison and the salvation of the jailer and his entire family.

The side-effect of FAITH in our God is PRAISE to Him.
The side-effect of PRAISE is HIS POWER! (ACTS 16:16-40)

## OWN MY SPACE
In Chaos, MY SPACE IS ORDER
In Crisis, MY SPACE IS PEACE

## RESPONDING TO CRISIS
ADAPT! Adjust my thinking to fit how "things are" instead of being stuck in what I think it should be or what I want it to be.

## COMPENSATE
Seek to make up the difference for what I lack and gain more.

## DON'T MISS THE POINT!
Too much emphasis on the crisis, and I miss the richness of working through the experience with Christ Jesus.
I can practice:
    1. Knowing Him better.
    2. Practicing taking off my old self and learning to wear my new self.
    3. Realizing my capabilities in Him.

## CRISIS MISBEHAVIORS
"I will forever be fascinated by how people deal with adversity, how people react in moments of crisis, or how people behave when life gets uncomfortable." –FORMER CHAMPION SOCCER PLAYER JULIE FOUDY

I share the same fascination and, sometimes, exasperation.

## REVISITING MINDSET
Although we know adversity is a common and frequent occurrence of life and living:
1. We wonder why us?
2. Don't prepare for it.
3. React emotionally rather than responding logically.
4. Easily fold from the weight of the "circumstances," which often paints a bleaker picture than it is, rather than believe what the Lord has promised.
5. Have amnesia, quickly forgetting how the Lord Jesus graced us through the last 18,888 times! Like He can't or won't do it again?

6. Convinced ourselves that it is TEOTWAWKI (Acronym for "the end of the world as we know it."), when it isn't.
7. Make no effort in developing the coping skills to adapt quickly to being uncomfortable.
8. Instead of harnessing what the Lord has already provided in and around us, reinforce our dependency on others.
9. Fret over tomorrow's adversity when tomorrow hasn't been promised to us, yet failing to acknowledge and enjoying today's blessings.

## "DON'T YOU PANIC!" LEARN & SERVE
Adversity is often the Kingdom's teaching and learning methodology used to promote my training and development in ministry to those in my area of operation.

I have to operate in my God-reality:
1.   Being mindful of His capability to assess what's going on.
2.   Drawing on His provisions for my needs.
3.   Being focused on working with Him to tend to the needs of others.

Worry, obsession and greed draw us farther from the Kingdom's provisions. (LUKE 12:29-34)

## MY STRESS RESPONSE
It took me quite a few years to get it (because I'm kinda slow on the uptake). Still, I've realized that my ability to make good decisions under stress results from being mindful of who I am and to whom I belong. Look to the Lord. (ISAIAH 41:13)

## INVITING PEACE
I cannot expect Peace to accept my invitations to where I have already invited Fear and Impatience. The Lord has sent peace. I did not make room for the others. (JOHN 14:27)

## WHAT SHOULD I FEEL?
When I need help centering my emotions, I pray:
> *Father, please help me not be afraid or to be terrorized when*
> *I have to face a critical event.*
> *Please help me to be aware of your presence, your power,*
> *your confidence, your indignation, your righteous anger,*
> *and your affection.*

And then I pause and reflect: What does Father feel? Make sure that it is made welcome.

## CALL OF DUTY

**Emergencies:**

It provides an opportunity for me to be the person I need to be.

I am presently involved in this situation because Father wants me to be there, and because He wants me there, He is trusting me with the tools and skills to handle it.

## SPIRITUAL READINESS:

The condition of awareness of the Father's presence, prepared, capable, and ready to execute His will on behalf of those who need His help.

## THE EYE OF THE STORM:

No matter how violent and destructive a hurricane is, peace is always in the center because the strong surface winds that meet up towards the center never reach it. In the same way, here is where my peace abides, and from here is where my capabilities flow.

# TRAINING & DEVELOPMENT

## YOU REAP WHAT YOU SOW

I became a police officer in the early 1980s. This period was significant because it was the beginning of the crack cocaine epidemic in New Jersey, where I lived.

I wasn't new to the streets of the City of Plainfield, where I served. Still, the wave of criminal behaviors that presented itself during that time was spooky.

At some point, right after getting out of the police academy, I often made and lived this proclamation, "No matter what, I'm going home." I was committed to doing EVERYTHING within my power to make sure that I would make it home at the end of my shift alive every day, the Lord willing.

I was trained to the state of New Jersey's standard for law enforcement officers. Still, I knew from my own street experience I was not trained in law enforcement street survival skills.

Even before the police department, I was already involved in martial arts at the time and training in firearms tactics.

I continued to do so on my own, outside the department's training program, with my own money on my own time.

Even back then, in my Heathenistic way, I trusted the Lord to protect me. Still, I also did my part because I understood that if I wanted the desired outcome.

"No matter what, I'm going home."

I had to make sure I trained to do what it took to get there.

> "How you train is how it will come out."
> – MARTIAL ARTS AND SELF-DEFENSE INSTRUCTOR DAVID JAMES[6]

---

6 https://www.vajjujitsu.com/about-vaj.html

# WISDOM FOR SURVIVAL

### I AM EMPTY SO THAT I CAN BE FILLED
I am first to admit that there are still a lot of basic facts I am totally ignorant of.

### HYPE IS NO SUBSTITUTE FOR KNOWLEDGE
An ignorant person who is not open to learning but is really hyped about doing something they know nothing about is often a train wreck with an upcoming appointment.

### BLOOD, SWEAT, AND TEARS
I can attend the best training classes money can buy and watch hundreds of training videos to learn how to defeat my internal/external enemies. Nonetheless, there will never be a better way to *truly know my enemy* until I go into the ring for a few rounds with them myself.

I no longer wonder why the Lord allows me to endure those dark times of pain and suffering.

How else will I know how to support the rescue and recovery of others? God brings us comfort so that we can provide it to others and to wait on his comfort. (2 CORINTHIANS 1:4)

### PRAYER FOR WISDOM
> *It angers me to consider how many years I was trained by foul spirits how to respond to life. Thank you, Lord Jesus, for loving me out of bondage.*

### HIS DAILY MASTER CLASS
I make it my business to be in the Holy Spirit's class daily for a good portion of the day. The Holy Spirit was sent to remind us of the lessons Jesus wanted us to learn to have a deeper relationship with the Father. (JOHN 14:26, 1 JOHN 2:27)

### COME READY TO LEARN, NOT READY TO TEACH/PREACH
I only expect to know the whole message after preaching/teaching it. During the message, I will get the rest of it along with everyone else.

### FEED THE HUNGRY
I have learned to stop trying to feed people that aren't hungry. In no time at all, I become a bother to them. On the other hand, hungry people will do whatever it takes to eat.

The religious person studies the Bible, and the spiritual person lives it.

## HIDDEN TREASURES

Just because someone has extensive experience doing something does not necessarily make them an expert. We may need to find out if they have been doing it correctly. Nonetheless, I would be very foolish not to listen and evaluate what they have to say.

It occurs to me that only those with a destination are concerned about course corrections.

I firmly believe that my personal experience does not have to be "the best teacher" when I can learn from someone else's experience safely and securely.

However, most of us prefer the "following the tracks of an overturned cart" method as a legitimate learning tool.

There have been many Scriptures and many prophets who have given us a guide for wisdom. (ROMANS 15:4)

When I am studying, the Holy Spirit is preaching and teaching me what's in the heart of God. I must have the heart of a student, assuming to know nothing so that something can be deposited in me. (JOHN 14:24-26)

"We don't rise to the level of our expectations; we fall to the level of our training." — ARCHILOCHUS

# Common sense is only common
# to those with the same reference point.

# OTHER NON-FICTION TITLES FROM PARISIAN PHOENIX

## Stops Along The Way
### By Charles Ticho

Charles Ticho—Czech born and a dual citizen of the United States and Israel—writes about his life in Europe, Israel and America, as a Holocaust survivor, film & commercial producer/director, world traveler and family historian. This memoir, published months before his death at 95, compiles many of his short essays, some new and some reworked from stories published in multiple global publications, including the *Jerusalem Post*. Ticho explores family, culture and Jewish history with his unique first person perspective.

## TWISTS: Gathered Ephemera
### By darrell parry

*Webster's Dictionary* defines Ephemera as, "something with no lasting significance."

The poems in this collection have been swept together from decades of open mics and feature performances, and pressed between these pages like fallen leaves like something fleeting, now preserved.

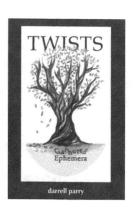

This book is the first full-length poetry collection from poet, artist and spoken-word performer Darrell Parry. Complete with nifty drawings and sage bits of wisdom scattered throughout, Twists offers a glimpse into a world of social anxiety and awkwardness with the experience and wisdom to accept an epic unknowing of everything.

**REVISED AND EXPANDED
SECOND EDITION NOW AVAILABLE**

# Not an Able-Bodied White Man with Money:

*Expressions of Alternative Perspectives Influenced by Experiences in Lehigh Valley, Pennsylvania*

Edited by Angel R. Ackerman

An identity politics anthology, *Not an Able-Bodied White Man with Money* features authors,poets, and artists selected not based on their writing ability, but for their ideas. The anthology features marginalized perspectives about LGBTQ issues, body image, disability, neurodivergence, ethnic backgrounds, mental health and much more.

## parisian phoenix
PUBLISHING

Purchase our titles on our website, online or ask for them at your favorite bookseller.

CPSIA information can be obtained
at www.ICGtesting.com
Printed in the USA
BVHW042230130423
662353BV00019B/232